STUFF!

A Curious Collection

by Sandra Fenichel Asher

a play in one act

inspired by the creative

and community-building work

of the Adventure Stage Chicago Trailblazers

Commissioned by Adventure Stage Chicago

Uproar Theatrics

LICENSING & PRODUCTION INQUIRIES
Uproar Theatrics, LLC.
hello@uproartheatrics.com | www.UproarTheatrics.com

With love and gratitude to my playwriting colleagues for their faith, inspiration, encouragement, splendid company, and, especially, for their stories.

The original Adventure Stage Chicago workshop production of STUFF! A Curious Collection was directed by Sarah Rose Graber with the following ensemble cast and crew of Trailblazers: Kevon Cosey, Paradise Cosey, Emilia Ferme, Leonardo Ferme, Nefrateri Figueroa, William Grove, Kimberly Gutierrez, Alyssa Vera Ramos, Matthew Scott, Jarrod Bainter, Laura B. Kollar, Melinda Kraus-Perrotta, Kenny Males, Anne McNamee, and Kamaya Thompson. Special thanks to guiding lights Allison Latta Lashford, Associate Artistic Director and Tom Arvetis, Artistic Director.

A full production by Creative Works Lancaster (PA) followed under the direction of Erin Brubaker. The cast, in order of appearance:

Penny Wrenn as Master of Creativity

Holly Andrew as Stuff

Melina Stratigos as Some One

Rachael Opendaker as Any One

Francisco Ortiz as Each One

Miranda Waldvogel as Every One

Abby Golden as Other One

STUFF!
A CURIOUS COLLECTION

CHARACTERS:

May be played by actors representing whatever variations of human being are locally available. All are welcome. Cast size is flexible.

M.C., (Master of Creativity), the embodiment of the human drive to find purpose, community and healing through shared stories. Upbeat, confident, and welcoming.

STUFF, non-speaking personification of odds and ends of absolutely no significance except when paired with human creativity. Wears a black jumpsuit or other comfortable, neutral outfit. In this play, as in life, STUFF calls to us, teases us, tickles us, troubles us, inspires us – and, in so doing, evokes the human creativity required to realize its own potential.

THE ONES:

SOME ONE, upper teens, loves to read and write stories. Also plays story characters MINEY, TRAVEL AGENT, LARRY, PUPPET CURLY, PUPPET MOE.

ANY ONE, early teens, a visual artist who loves to play dress-up and finds costume pieces for others as indicated. Also plays story character MOTHER.

EACH ONE, a drummer who loves to play with all kinds of sound and helps to create sound effects as indicated. Also plays story characters FATHER, LION, PUPPET WHALE.

EVERY ONE, upper teens, born to dance.
Also plays the story characters MEENY, TOUR GUIDE

OTHER ONE, the youngest of the ONES, grieving for a
beloved pet.
Also plays story character EENY, and shares operation of
PUPPET MOE

NOTE: For a larger cast, STORY CHARACTERS may be
played by additional actors, with or without use of puppets,
all imagined into being by the ONES as they create their
group story. STUFF's role can be divided among additional
actors, all non-speaking, either as equals or as assistants to a
single leading STUFF.

STUFF is always aware of the M.C., the audience, the
ONES, and the STORY CHARACTERS. ONES and
STORY CHARACTERS are not aware of the M.C., the
audience, or STUFF. STUFF needs human beings to create
its significance, so it takes pains to include the audience in
whatever it's doing. Except when inside the container,
STUFF is always visible to the audience, but invisible to the
ONES. SOUND produced by STUFF is experienced by
ONES as if it were their own idea or memory.

PLACE: Anywhere. Here.

TIME: Any time. Now.

RUNNING TIME: about 50 minutes

M.C.
(to audience)
Greetings, one and all. Welcome . . . to this dump.
(indicates sign)
Which dump is it? Well, it could be anywhere. Any time.
Except that it's . . .
(turns sign to read HERE. NOW.)
Here. Now. And it could remain a simple dump . . . except
that I'm also here now. That makes all the difference.
(beat)
Who am I? I am the M.C., which usually means "Master of
Ceremonies." But I am more than Master of Ceremonies. I
am Master of Creativity.
(a gracious bow --)
At your service. My job is to turn this dump into a recycling
center. Not THAT kind of recycling. Not old plastic bottles
into new park benches or old newspapers into new kitty
litter. I'm all in favor of that kind of recycling. It's very
creative. But *this* is something else entirely. Because this is
a dump for people. People who are down in the dumps.
(nods while that sinks in, then --)

1

                                M.C. (CONT)
Well! I've got work to do. Fortunately, I am not alone.
Enter . . . *Stuff*! . . .

> *(STUFF appears at the top of the dumpster,*
> *looks around, notes audience with pleasure,*
> *emerges from the dumpster to toy with the debris*
> *on stage, offering this and that in an effort to*
> *please the M.C., who ponders --)*

Old stuff . . . broken stuff . . . silly stuff . . .
> *(to audience)*
But never, never, useless stuff. You'll see.
> *(beat)*
Hmmmmm. Where to begin? So much stuff, so little time.

> *(A large, blank BOOK appears magically.*
> *Perhaps it's lowered from above or pulled across*
> *downstage or discovered in some unexpected*
> *place. There is a PLUME-like pen attached to*
> *it or tucked inside.)*

Ah! More help has arrived!
> *(to STUFF)*
Fascinating, don't you think?
> *(STUFF shrugs, unsure what it thinks, since stuff*
> *never does think.)*
Of course.
> *(to audience)*
I do the thinking. Stuff does the doing. As it should be.
Let's get started!

> *(M.C. claps or waves STUFF into action, then*
> *watches with approval and occasional*
> *encouraging gestures, as STUFF takes up*
> *BOOK and PLUME, examines them, mimes*
> *asking the audience if they belong to any*

one. They do not. What to do with them?
STUFF shows inside of BOOK to audience in a
general way, indicating that the pages are
empty. Then, on a whim, STUFF holds the open
book out toward individual audience members
more intentionally, waving PLUME over the
chosen one's head, then snapping BOOK shut
each time as if capturing something. Each time,
the next opening of the book produces a
satisfying SOUND, as if the audience member's
thought has been recorded and played
back. The first SOUND is a LION's roar, much
to STUFF's delight and M.C.'s approval.
STUFF then closes BOOK, ending that SOUND,
waves PLUME and opens BOOK toward
another audience member. Closes BOOK,
opens it, and out comes a WHALE-like moaning
SOUND. Business is repeated and results in the
yapping of a DOG, and, finally, a lilting, bell-
like MELODY. Pleased, STUFF leaves BOOK
open to that page and plays it back to the
dumpster, then shuts BOOK and disappears
inside with it.)

                    M.C.
Excellent stuff! And now . . . it's time to meet the Ones.
          (a beat, then --)
Enter . . . Some One!

          (ONES enter one at a time, as announced by
          M.C., dressed plainly, in neutral colors. Their
          garb will become more colorful as they add bits
          and pieces of "stuff" in the course of the play.
          In turn, each crisscrosses the stage repeatedly,
          ignoring the dumpster, the debris, the sign, the
          M.C., and the other ONES while absorbed in
          chanting the trivia of everyday life. ALL stride

3

in a rigid manner and intone their words
with monotonous intensity, trapped in an
apparently numbing and never-ending daily
routine.)

SOME ONE
(enters, crisscrosses stage, chanting --)
Bedroom . . . light switch . . . hallway . . . bathroom . . . light
switch . . . hallway . . . stairs living room . . . shelf . . .
(A tiny pause, a brightening, but with a sense of
longing --)
Book!
(a shudder, then trudging on --)
Hallway . . . door . . . sidewalk . . . street . . .

(SOME ONE continues crisscrossing stage and
repeats the above chant more softly but
otherwise in the exact same way as ANY ONE
enters.)

M.C.
Enter . . . Any One!

ANY ONE
(enters, crisscrosses stage, chanting --)
Steps . . . sidewalk . . . street . . . bus . . . sidewalk . . .
steps . . . hallway . . . locker . . . hallway . . . door . . .
hallway . . . hallway . . . door . . .
(A tiny pause, brightening, but with a sense of
longing --)
Art room!
(a shudder, then trudging on --)
Chair . . . desk . . . hallway . . . door . . .

(ANY ONE continues crisscrossing stage and
repeats the above chant more softly but

4

otherwise in the exact same way as EACH ONE enters.)

M.C.

Enter . . . Each One!

EACH ONE
(enters, crisscrosses stage, chanting --)
Cafeteria . . . line . . . tray . . . counter . . . table . . . trash . . . door . . . hallway . . . door . . .
(a tiny pause, brightening, but with a sense of longing --)
Music room!
(a shudder, then trudging on --)
Locker . . . door . . . gym . . . locker . . . door . . .

(EACH ONE continues crisscrossing stage and repeats the above chant more softly but otherwise in the exact same way as EVERY ONE enters.)

M.C.

Enter . . . Every One!

EVERY ONE
(enters, crisscrosses stage, chanting --)
Bus . . . door . . . steps . . . aisle . . . seat . . . window . . . aisle . . . steps . . . sidewalk . . . store window . . . store window . . .
(a tiny pause, brightening, but with a sense of longing --)
Dance studio!
(a shudder, then trudging on --)
Store window . . . store window . . . store window . . .

(EVERY ONE continues crisscrossing stage and repeats the above chant more softly but

                    otherwise in the exact same way as OTHER
                    ONE enters.)

                              M.C.
Enter . . . Other One!

                          OTHER ONE
                    (enters, crisscrosses stage, chanting --)
Hallway . . . light switch . . . bedroom . . . closet . . . bed . . .
blanket . . . pillow . . .
                    (a joyless pause -- "Is this all there is?"-- then,
                    with a sigh of resignation --)
Wall.

                    (ALL except OTHER ONE freeze. OTHER ONE
                    abruptly sinks to knees, as if facing an
                    insurmountable wall and freezes. In turn, each
                    of the ONES does the same, each in his or her
                    own space, facing different walls in different
                    directions, still unaware of one another.)

                          EVERY ONE
                    (sinking to floor)
Wall.

                          EACH ONE
                    (sinking to floor)
Wall.

                          ANY ONE
                    (sinking to floor)
Wall.

                          SOME ONE
                    (sinking to floor)
Wall.

                    (ONES freeze.)

M.C.

Uh-oh. The Ones have hit The Wall. The Big Shrug. The Why Bother? The Whatever.

> *(beat)*

The Wall.

> *(beat)*

Next stop? Down in the dumps . . .

> *(beat)*

. . . where we refresh, refuel, restore . . .

> *(beat)*

In short, where stuff happens!

> *(At M.C.'s signal, STUFF pops up from dumpster, look at ONES, at audience, at ONES again, then emerges from dumpster, cautiously stepping around each of the frozen ONES and eyeing each with concern, then looks at M.C., "What to do?" M.C. responds with a signal. STUFF grins at audience, disappears into container, quickly re-emerges with five large cubes, and arranges them in a straight line, left to right, downstage of the ONES, spaced at even distances from one another. The cubes are all the same neutral color. That done, STUFF shoots M.C. another "What now?"look. M.C. signals, STUFF grins again at audience, then retrieves BOOK and PLUME from the container.)*

M.C.

Stuff plus Ones. Reconstruct, relate, respond . . .

> *(With one last signal to STUFF, M.C. takes an out-of-the way seat, joins the audience to watch what ensues, or exits. At this point, M.C. may continue as an offstage voice, or may pop in from unexpected places as needed.*

*STUFF opens BOOK, and lays it on top of
the first cube at right. STUFF then waves
PLUME over SOME ONE's head. Although
SOME ONE has no idea where the impetus has
come from, a memory and a story are evoked.
SOMEONE stands and talks as STUFF sits near
first cube and listens sympathetically, including
the audience in this response. As each of the
following stories is told, the ONE telling it
becomes less robotic. Individual personalities
begin to break through.)*

SOME ONE
(thinking aloud, to no one in particular --)
I set my alarm for six-thirty. Plenty of time to catch the bus.
But Dad's running late. He's in a panic, and he needs his
coffee. I put in the filter. I measure the grounds. I add
water and press "start." Same as always. Then I go into my
bedroom to get dressed and I hear this
PPPPTTTTHHHHZZZZZZZZZZZZZZZZZZZ. I run back
to the kitchen and coffee's exploding out of the pot! First
thing I do is, I yank my books out of the way. Dad's so
desperate, he's holding his cup at the edge of the counter and
guiding spilled coffee into it. He's got to leave for work.
I've got to leave, too, but there's a *black coffee lake* on our
kitchen floor! I set my books down in a safe place, grab a
towel and mop it up, but now I'm stuck with this sopping
wet blob in my hands! I'm going to miss the bus! I drop the
towel in the sink, finish getting dressed, pick up my books,
and make a run for it. Too late. The bus is halfway up the
next block.
        (beat)
I could drive --
        (a shudder)
No. *No.*

(SOME ONE freezes. STUFF gently takes BOOK from the cube, notes that this story has been recorded on its pages, closes it, opens it. MELODY plays. SOME ONE reacts as if hearing it, but doesn't know where it's coming from. As STUFF uses BOOK and MELODY to lure SOME ONE forward --)

SOME ONE (CONT)
I begin walking . . . just walking . . . and all of a sudden . . .

(STUFF continues to lure SOME ONE forward until they reach the first cube. STUFF closes BOOK. MELODY fades.)

. . . I end up here.

(Disoriented, puzzled by the silence, SOME ONE sits, facing upstage, and freezes. STUFF grins again at audience, carries BOOK to second cube, and lays it on top, opened to a new page. STUFF then wavesPLUME over ANY ONE. ANY ONE has no idea where the impetus has come from, but a memory and a story are evoked. ANY ONE stands and talks as STUFF sits near the second cube and listens sympathetically, including the audience in this response.)

ANY ONE
(thinking aloud; to no one in particular --)
I can't sleep. I don't know why. I'm the only one in the house who's awake. So I get dressed and go outside. No one on the street. Silence. Dark shadows beyond the glow of the streetlamps. It feels as if I'm the only one in the entire world who's awake. Eerie. But I kind of like it. I get out my bike and ride around the neighborhood. *Around and around in*

ANY ONE (CONT)

circles. Still nobody. Just quiet, sleeping buildings, with shaded windows like closed eyes. Then it begins to get light. The sunrise is beautiful. I could paint this scene, I think. I could call it . . .

(a shudder, and then --)

No. *No.*

(ANY ONE freezes. STUFF takes BOOK from second cube, notes the newly recorded story, closes the book, opens it. MELODY plays. ANY ONE reacts as if hearing it, but doesn't know where it's coming from. As STUFF uses BOOK and MELODY to lure ANY ONE forward --)

And then . . . I start walking . . . and walking . . .

(STUFF continues to lure ANY ONE forward until they reach the second cube. STUFF closes book. MELODY fades.)

. . . and I come here.

(Disoriented, puzzled, ANY ONE takes a seat on second cube, facing upstage, and freezes. Pleased, STUFF carries BOOK to third cube, and lays it on top, open to a new page. STUFF then waves PLUME over EACH ONE. EACH ONE has no idea where the impetus comes from, but it evokes a memory and a story. EACH ONE stands and talks as STUFF sits near the third cube and listens sympathetically, including the audience in this response.)

EACH ONE
                (thinking aloud; to no one in particular --)
I wake up in a panic because my sister's in her room yelling,
"It's ten-thirty! It's ten-thirty!" I jump out of bed, my heart
pounding: KA-BOOM. KA-BOOM. KA-BOOM. Why
didn't my alarm go off? And then I finally look at my own
clock, and it says six-forty-three. "Hey!" I yell through the
wall, "My clock says six-forty-three . . . six-forty-four!" A
long silence. I punch the wall. THONK! THONK! "Hello?
Is it ten-thirty or six-forty-four?" "Ooops," she says. "I
must've pulled the wrong plug."
                (a beat, a roll of the eyes, then --)
And then my alarm goes off, at 6:45. I shower, I dress, I eat,
I leave. Halfway there, I realize I've forgotten my sheet
music for band practice. Again! How many times has it
been now? Why do I keep doing that? Should I go on
without it? Should I run back and get it?
                (looking one way, then the other)
No. *No.*

                *(EACH ONE freezes. STUFF takes BOOK from
                third cube, notes the recorded story, closes
                BOOK, opens it. MELODY plays. EACH ONE
                reacts as if hearing it, but doesn't know where
                it's coming from. As STUFF uses BOOK and
                MELODY to lure EACH ONE forward --)*

Next thing I know . . . I'm not going home . . . and I'm not
going to school . . .

                *(STUFF continues to lure EACH ONE forward
                until they reach the third cube. STUFF closes
                book. MELODY fades.)*

I'm here.
                *(Disoriented, puzzled, EACH ONE takes a seat
                on the third cube, facing upstage and freezes.*

STUFF carries BOOK to fourth cube, lays it on top, open, then waves PLUME over EVERY ONE. EVERY ONE has no idea where the impetus has come from, but a memory and a story are evoked. EVERY ONE stands and talks as STUFF sits near fourth cube and listens sympathetically, including the audience in this response.)

EVERY ONE
(thinking aloud, to no one in particular --)
Mom's already gone to work, but she's left me some *cornbread.* Mmmmm-mmmm! I pop it in the microwave, and figure I can be in and out of the shower and it'll be nice and warm. So I'm back in a flash and, sure enough, the whole place smells like *cornbread heaven.*
(establishing a rhythm –)
So now I'm eating cornbread, drying off, eating cornbread, fixing my hair, eating cornbread, getting dressed, eating cornbread, packing my lunch, eating cornbread, gathering my stuff . . .
(momentarily enjoying this "dance" –)
. . . nibble and dry . . . nibble and fix . . . nibble and dress . . . nibble and pack . . .
(abruptly stops as a wave of sadness rolls in)
Whoa. Uh-uh. No. *No.*

(EVERY ONE freezes. STUFF picks up BOOK, notes that the story has been entered, closes it, opens it. MELODY plays. EVERY ONE reacts as if hearing it, but doesn't know where it's coming from. As STUFF uses BOOK and MELODY to lure EVERY ONE forward --)

I go outside . . . Next thing I know . . . I'm walking . . . I don't know where . . .

*(STUFF continues to lure EVERY ONE forward
until they reach the fourth cube. STUFF closes
BOOK. MELODY fades.)*

EVERY ONE (CONT)

And I come here.

*(Disconcerted, puzzled, EVERY ONE takes a
seat on the fourth cube, facing upstage and
freezes. STUFF carries BOOK to fifth cube, lays
it on top, open, then waves PLUME over
OTHER ONE. OTHER ONE has no idea where
the impetus has come from. It flickers, and just
as quickly fades.)*

OTHER ONE
*(stands, thinking aloud; to no one in
particular--)*

I did not want to wake up this morning.
(beat, then sadly --)

No. *No.*

*(OTHER ONE freezes. Expecting a
story, STUFF is confused. STUFF shares this
with audience, and then there's nothing for it
except to try to move things along. A beat.
STUFF takes BOOK from fifth cube, notes
that not much has been entered, closes it,
opens it. MELODY plays. OTHER ONE
reacts as if hearing it, but doesn't know where
it's coming from. As STUFF uses BOOK and
MELODY to lure OTHER ONE forward --)*

So . . . I don't know . . . I just . . . I just end up here.

*(spins around to face upstage at fifth cube,
sits, and freezes. STUFF wanders from cube to*

13

cube, searching the ONES' faces for a clue as to
what to do next, then faces forward, shrugging
helplessly.)

                    M.C. (may be offstage voice)
Well, well! A bit puzzling, eh?
                    (STUFF nods "yes.")
Don't worry. There's all kinds of stuff left.

                    (STUFF brightens, puts down BOOK,
                    and begins to race around, picking up,
                    examining, and rearranging the miscellaneous
                    objects upstage and around the container. Some
                    of this stuff makes SOUNDS and perhaps casts
                    LIGHT. Have fun with that! Eventually, STUFF
                    is worn out with the effort, returns downstage to
                    BOOK and awaits instruction.)

Let's continue . . .
                    (beat)
Some One . . . Plus . . . Messy Stuff.

                    (STUFF selects a license plate from the debris,
                    smiles in approval, and delivers the license
                    plate to SOME ONE. Again, this is done without
                    SOME ONE realizing where the object has come
                    from. A beat, then SOME ONE unfreezes and,
                    without looking at STUFF, takes license plate,
                    turns forward, and finds it inspires the telling of
                    a story. STUFF sits and listens attentively,
                    holding the open BOOK and sharing that
                    interest with the audience.)

                    (NOTE: In this round of stories, the ONES fully
                    reveal the hurt in their hearts and become open
                    to one another.)

SOME ONE

I hit a kid with my car.

(ANY ONE unfreezes and takes guarded interest; remains seated but shifts around to observe SOME ONE, who continues facing downstage, clutching license plate.)

ANY ONE

Oh, wow!

SOME ONE

Well, actually, it's my dad's car. And I didn't exactly hit the kid. He kind of hit the car. With his whole body. Or maybe we hit one another. It was raining hard, and he was leaving the library, and I was heading into the parking lot. He was clutching a bunch of *books* -- hunched over, trying to keep them dry -- and he stepped into the street, right where I was making my turn. So I stopped. And then he stopped and tilted his head, like "Go on, go on." So I did, but he took another step. So then I'm like, "Go on, go on."
(beat)
Then he stopped again, so I pulled forward. But he moved at the same time and slammed right into the car.
(beat)
Or I hit him. I don't know. He wasn't hurt, just shook up, but he'd dropped all those books right into a puddle.
"They're *library* books!" he kept saying, "They're *library* books!" As if they were sacred. Which they are! I knew exactly how he felt. He was like this younger version of me, a bookworm, maybe even a writer, loving the library, loving those books. And we'd ruined them.
(beat)
I didn't even get a ticket, but I felt as if I should've gone to jail.

ANY ONE

At least the kid wasn't hurt.

SOME ONE

But there were *the books* . . .

ANY ONE

Well, that is bad —

SOME ONE

I know!

ANY ONE

It was an accident.

SOME ONE
(with a shrug; not entirely convinced --)
Thank you.

ANY ONE

You're welcome.

SOME ONE
(quietly)
I stopped driving. I haven't been back to the library. Which
is weird, because I practically lived there. But . . . I can't.

*(Both ANY ONE and STUFF react with
sympathetic concern. STUFF checks that the
story is in BOOK, then closes it. Through
the next stories, SOME ONE and ANY ONE
continue to warm to one another.)*

M.C. (may be offstage voice)
Any One . . . Plus . . . Hurtful Stuff.

*(STUFF quickly retrieves two dolls and brings
them to ANY ONE. ANY ONE takes the
dolls without understanding where they came
from and is inspired to tell a story. STUFF sits
and listens, holding the open BOOK.)*

ANY ONE

I don't like it when people hurt people. I don't mean
accidents. I mean on purpose. It makes me crazy.

*(EACH ONE unfreezes and takes guarded
interest, remaining seated while shifting around
to observe ANY ONE, who continues facing
downstage, clutching dolls protectively.)*

EACH ONE

Yeah, me, too.

ANY ONE

My sister and I used to go to the park near our house with
our sketch pads and colored pencils. We'd dress ourselves
up in these wild hats and scarves, pretending we were
famous artists, and talking with *French accents*. One day,
we were sitting on a bench, just drawing pictures and
minding our own business, when this kid from school started
picking on us. My sister is really shy. This guy's in her
class and I knew he sometimes picked on her at school, but
this was the weekend. Give it a break! She was drawing a
tree. He said it looked like a *whale*. And then he said it
must've been a self-portrait because *she* looked like a whale!
It made me so mad, I could hardly see straight. I jumped off
the bench and rushed toward him -- *roaring*, like a *lion*!
       (furiously and ferociously)
RRRRROOOOAAAARRRRRRRRRR!
       (beat)
I don't know why I did that. Neither did he. He took off
running!

EACH ONE

Good for you!

ANY ONE

It was crazy! I didn't think . . . I just did it!

EACH ONE

You stood up for your sister. That's good.

ANY ONE
(with a shrug; not entirely convinced --)

Thank you.

EACH ONE

You're welcome.

ANY ONE
(shrugs; shakes her head)

Kids at school heard about it. The roaring. The outfits. The
French accent. The teasing got worse. For both of us . . .
(beat)
We don't dress up anymore. She stopped drawing. So did I.

> *(STUFF sympathizes and closes BOOK.
> SOME ONE, ANY ONE, and EACH ONE
> continue to relate to one another in small, shy
> ways.)*

M.C. (may be offstage voice)

Each One . . . Plus . . . Scary Stuff.

> *(STUFF retrieves a steering wheel and delivers
> it to EACH ONE. Without seeing STUFF, EACH
> ONE takes the wheel, turns forward, and tells a
> story. SOME ONE and ANY ONE, respond with*

*interest. STUFF sits and listens, holding open
BOOK.)*

EACH ONE

I was waiting for the bus after school. There was this girl
and she was carrying an instrument in *a battered case*, a
viola.

*(EVERY ONE unfreezes and shifts around to
face EACH ONE.)*

EVERY ONE

What's a viola?

EACH ONE

Like a violin, only bigger.

EVERY ONE

Oh. Okay.

EACH ONE

She must've been on her way to City Youth Orchestra. There
were these guys – a bunch of them – waiting for the same
bus. They were fooling around, punching one another,
yelling and laughing. The bus came. We all got on. The girl
took a seat next to an older man and one of those guys sat
down across the aisle from her. I was two rows back. I
could hear him asking her questions like "Hey! What's in
there? Your lunch? Must be rotten by now!" She explained,
politely, but the other guys were cracking up at everything
she said. I wanted to tell them to stop, but I was just one kid
and they were *big*. I thought the man next to her would say
something, but he just sat there. The guy went on asking
stupid questions and his friends went on laughing and even
when they finally got off the bus, they banged on her
window and made faces. That's when she finally burst into

EACH ONE (CONT)
tears. How is it possible that everybody saw what was
happening and nobody did anything?   Including me?

EVERY ONE
You were scared. You were outnumbered.

EACH ONE
(with a shrug; not entirely convinced --)
Thank you.

EVERY ONE
You're welcome.

EACH ONE
(quietly)
I used to dream about joining City Youth Orchestra, but,
now, I don't know . . .

*(SOME ONE, ANY ONE, EACH ONE, and
EVERY ONE continue showing interest in
one another in shy ways. STUFF closes book.
A beat, then --)*

M.C. (may be offstage voice)
Every One . . . Plus . . . Bad Stuff.

*(STUFF retrieves a stethoscope and delivers it
to EVERY ONE, who takes it without knowing
where it came from and tells story. All ONES
respond with shy interest, except for OTHER
ONE, who is still facing upstage. STUFF sits
and listens, holding open BOOK.)*

EVERY ONE

I was at the hospital when my grandfather died.   He was in the Intensive Care Unit.

> *(OTHER ONE unfreezes at the word "died" and takes interest, remaining seated while shifting to face EVERY ONE.)*

They don't let people visit.

OTHER ONE

No one at all?

EVERY ONE

They let adults. They don't let kids. I really wanted to see my Grandpa!
> *(ALL murmur agreement; STUFF
> nods sympathetically. A beat, then --)*

He was a *dancer*. He and my grandma won contests. When I was little, I'd put my feet on top of his and he'd dance me around. That's how it began. He taught me all kinds of dances. He came to every one of my shows.
> *(a beat, remembering that, then --)*

There was a big glass window in that waiting room, with doctors and nurses on the other side who didn't even look at me, not even once. I wanted to pick up a chair and throw it through the glass. But I had to just sit there.

OTHER ONE

Were you crying?

EVERY ONE

When I wasn't too busy being angry.
> *(a beat, then --)*

My aunt came out after a while, really crying hard, and a couple minutes later, my mom came out and told us kids that Grandpa had died.

OTHER ONE
I'm so sorry.
>   (*OTHERS nod and murmur in agreement.*)

EVERY ONE
>   (*with a shrug; not entirely comforted --)*
Thank you.

OTHER ONE
You're welcome.

EVERY ONE
>   (*quietly*)
I don't ever . . . I don't want to . . . dance anymore . . .

>   (*As before, STUFF responds to EVERY ONE'S
>   mood sympathetically while closing BOOK. A
>   beat, then --)*

M.C.
Other One . . . Plus . . . Sad Stuff.

>   (*STUFF retrieves a dog leash and, after a bit of
>   deliberation considering OTHER ONE'S
>   attitude, delivers it to OTHER ONE, who takes
>   it without knowing where it came from. A long
>   pause, while STUFF and ONES anxiously await
>   a response. Then OTHER ONE sighs
>   deeply. STUFF and ONES sigh deeply. ALL
>   wait, eyes on OTHER ONE. Finally, OTHER
>   ONE speaks.STUFF sits and opens BOOK --)*

OTHER ONE
I did not want to wake up this morning.

SOME ONE

Why not?

OTHER ONE

Because I thought maybe if I didn't open my eyes, my dog would still be there, next to my bed, where she's always been, every single morning of my entire life. But I couldn't just lie there forever – and I knew she was gone. She will never be there again . . . never . . . ever . . . again. *No more!* No more licking my face to say "Good morning." No more racing me downstairs to breakfast. No more bouncing around my feet, excited to go out for a walk. *No more . . .* soft . . . warm . . . happy . . . anything.

SOME ONE

I'm sorry.
          (OTHERS nod and murmur in agreement.)

OTHER ONE
          (a shrug; not at all comforted --)
Thanks.

SOME ONE

You're welcome.

OTHER ONE

Mom says we can get another dog, but I don't want *another* dog!
          (a beat; then tossing the leash to the ground --)
I want *my* dog. I will never . . . love . . . *anything* . . . or . . . *anyone* . . . ever . . . ever . . .again! No! No more! *No . . . more.*

          (An awkward pause, as ONES sneak peeks at one another and exchange shrugs, unsure of what to do next. STUFF closes book, looks at audience, wide-eyed with concern.)

M.C. (may be offstage voice)
(a beat, then --)
Well! Time to move on . . . to new stuff. Rearrange . . .
reinvest . . . rebuild . . .

> *(STUFF agrees that something new is
> needed. STUFF whisks objects away from
> SOME ONE, ANY ONE, EACH ONE, EVERY
> ONE, and OTHER ONE, respectively, and sets
> them aside. ONES are aware of things being
> removed, but not of how or why. They sputter in
> astonishment.)*

SOME ONE
Wait a second . . . ! Didn't I just have a . . . ?

ANY ONE
That was . . . odd . . . ! I could've sworn I . . .

EACH ONE
Did you see that . . . ? I was holding a . . .

EVERY ONE
What in the world . . . ? Where did that go . . . ?

OTHER ONE
What? How did . . . ? Did you see . . . ?

> *(While the ONES are trying to figure out where
> those objects went, STUFF yanks the cubes out
> from under each of them, one after another.
> SOME ONE and EVERY ONE stagger but land
> on their feet. ANY ONE EACH ONE, and
> OTHER ONE topple to the ground and have to
> be helped up.)*

SOME ONE

Hey!

ANY ONE

Whoa!

EACH ONE

Whaaaa?

EVERY ONE

Whooops!

OTHER ONE

Yikes!

*(Now ONES are facing one another, brushing
themselves and each other off, sharing their
confusion.)*

M.C. (may be offstage voice)
All right! All together now . . . revise . . . re-envision . . .
reignite . . .

*(With the cubes either back in the container
or out of the way, STUFF moves quickly to pick
up new objects from the ground – not the props
already already used -- and tosses them into the
circle of ONES. ONES catch them without
knowing where they've come from and toss them
back and forth to one another in "hot potato"
alarm at first. Soon ONES' movements become
less driven by unknown forces and more playful
until at last they're laughing and
shouting encouragement to one another, ad
libbing "Here!" "Catch!" "Your turn!" "Heads
up!" etc. Eventually, their tosses become
controlled and rhythmic and they begin chanting*

"hip, hup, hip, hup" in a synchronized exchange of objects. Then STUFF reaches into the game, unseen, and removes objects one catch at a time until they're all out of the game, to STUFF'S amusement and the ONES' consternation.)

ONES
(tossing fewer and fewer objects --)
Hip! . . . Hup! . . . Hip! . . . Hup! . . . Hip! . . . Hup! . . . Hip! . . . Hup . . . HUH?

(As ONES suddenly find themselves empty-handed, their chant fades away to a puzzled silence.)

ANY ONE
Would someone please tell me what just happened? What is going on here?

SOME ONE
Whatever it is, I kinda like it.

EACH ONE
Me, too.

EVERY ONE
Me, three.

OTHER ONE
You all like it?

EACH ONE, SOME ONE, EVERY ONE
(one word each, overlapping one another --)
Yeah. Sorta. Kinda.

ANY ONE
(to OTHER ONE)

Don't you?

OTHER ONE

Well . . . maybe . . .

SOME ONE

I wonder what's going to happen next?

*(ONES look at one another, all wondering,
shrugging, looking around expectantly. STUFF,
also, except STUFF relates to audience and
hears M.C.)*

M.C. (may be offstage voice)

What's going to happen next? *More stuff!* Restructure . . .
repurpose . . . reinvent . . .

*(Immediately inspired, STUFF picks up BOOK
and hands it to SOME ONE, then invites
audience to watch as the story unfolds. SOME
ONE receives BOOK without knowing where it
came from and is intrigued and delighted by it.
In the same way that SOME ONE takes the lead
in creating the story and ANY ONE contributes
to the story by adding costume bits and pieces,
ways should be found for EACH ONE to add
sound effects, for EVERY ONE to turn
movement into dance, and for OTHER ONE to
demonstrate a special affinity for animals.)*

SOME ONE

Hey! How about a story?

ANY ONE

What?

                    EVERY ONE
What story?

                    EACH ONE
A story about what?

                    SOME ONE
                    (opens BOOK; shows blank pages)
About whatever we want.

                    EVERY ONE
                    (picks up dolls and dances them about)
Okay. A family.

                    EACH ONE
                    *(picks up steering wheel and a horn to honk or
                    bicycle bell to ring)*
A family going on a trip.

                    ANY ONE
                    (adding scraps of costume to the dolls)
Yes!
                    (to OTHER ONE)
Come on! Help us!

                    OTHER ONE
Do I have to?

                    ANY ONE
No. You don't have to. But it'll be more fun if you do.

                    OTHER ONE
Oh . . . okay.
                    *(OTHER ONE shrugs and gets busy, to ANY
                    ONE'S approval.)*

SOME ONE
(pretending to read from BOOK)
Once upon a time, there was a family that wanted to go on
vacation.
(SOME ONE looks at page with surprise.)
Oh!

EVERY ONE
Oh, what?

SOME ONE
What I say is turning up in this book!

(Other ONES and STUFF peer in at page.)

EVERY ONE
Wow!

EACH ONE
Well, let's keep going . . .

*(ONES form a FAMILY without regard
to appropriate size or gender. EACH ONE picks
up the steering wheel and as ONES are assigned
their FAMILY positions, they scramble into
place as passengers in a car.)*

ANY ONE
(finds costume scraps for herself and dons them)
A mother –

EACH ONE
(accepting costume scraps from ANY ONE)
A father –

                    ANY ONE
And their three beloved children –
                    (pulling in OTHER ONE --)
Eeny –

                    *(hands dolls to OTHER ONE, whom she also
                    decks out in costume scraps. As the ONES enter
                    the world of their story, they find voices, stances,
                    and gestures to suit their newly minted
                    characters. Pulling in EVERY ONE --)*

Meeny . . .
                    (Pulling in SOME ONE --)
 . . . and Miney.

                    OTHER ONE
No Moe?

                    ANY ONE
No Moe.

                    OTHER ONE
                    (saddened by this)
Oh.

                    EACH ONE as FATHER
Okay, Family, where shall we go on our vacation trip?

                    ANY ONE as MOTHER
How about the beach?

                    EVERY ONE as MEENY
Uh-uh. The city!

                    SOME ONE as MINEY
Why not the mountains?

OTHER ONE as EENY

No! The zoo!
>   *(a backseat argument breaks out among the*
>   *"children.")*

M.C. (may be offstage voice)

Hold on there!
>   *(ONES freeze.)*
This Family needs a travel agent.

>   *(STUFF agrees, takes BOOK from SOME ONE*
>   *and replaces it with a folded map and a battered*
>   *viola case. ONES unfreeze.)*

Enter . . . Travel Agent.

SOME ONE as TRAVEL AGENT

Greetings, Family. I am a travel agent!

ANY ONE as MOTHER
>   *(immediately adds a wide-brimmed hat to SOME*
>   *ONE's TRAVEL AGENT)*
How lucky is that?

SOME ONE as TRAVEL AGENT

In-your-wildest-dreams lucky!
>   *(unfolds map)*
I just happen to have an extremely exclusive, incredibly
inclusive, and consistently conducive tour for you.

OTHER ONE as EENY

Conducive to what?

SOME ONE as TRAVEL AGENT

That depends.

                    OTHER ONE as EENY
On what?

                    SOME ONE as TRAVEL AGENT
On you.

                    OTHER ONE as EENY
On us?

                    ANY ONE as MOTHER
                    (gently moving OTHER ONE out of the way)
Please tell us all about it.

                    SOME ONE as TRAVEL AGENT
I can't.

                    ANY ONE as MOTHER
Why not?

                    SOME ONE as TRAVEL AGENT
It's a secret.

                    EVERY ONE as MEENY
Oooh, an undisclosed destination!

                    EACH ONE as FATHER
But you've taken this tour before, right?

                    SOME ONE as TRAVEL AGENT
I can't tell you that, either.

                    OTHER ONE as EENY
Why not?

                    SOME ONE as TRAVEL AGENT
Because I haven't.

EVERY ONE as MEENY
You've never taken this tour?

SOME ONE as TRAVEL AGENT
No.

ANY ONE as MOTHER
But it comes highly recommended?

SOME ONE as TRAVEL AGENT
Not really.

OTHER ONE as EENY
Why not?

SOME ONE as TRAVEL AGENT
Because no one else has ever taken it before.

ANY ONE as MOTHER
No one?

SOME ONE as TRAVEL AGENT
No one. Ever.

EACH ONE as FATHER
You did say it was exclusive . . .

SOME ONE as TRAVEL AGENT
Extremely.

ANY ONE as MOTHER
And inclusive.

SOME ONE as TRAVEL AGENT
Incredibly.

OTHER ONE as EENY
And conducive . . .

SOME ONE as TRAVEL AGENT
Consistently.

OTHER ONE as EENY
But you don't know anything about it --

ANY ONE as MOTHER
(gently moving OTHER ONE out of the way)
I say we do it!   We'll be adventurers!

EVERY ONE as MEENY
Explorers!

EACH ONE as FATHER
Trailblazers!

OTHER ONE as EENY
(with concern)
Or . . . something. But *what*?

(SOME ONE as TRAVEL AGENT opens viola case, which is empty, puts it on the ground, and waits expectantly. A beat, while ONES look at each other blankly. SOME ONE as TRAVEL AGENT points emphatically at the case with much loud throat-clearing, and glares at ONES impatiently. ONES finally realize what's being requested. With cries of "Oh!" and "Aha!" and "Of course!" ONES hurriedly gather miscellaneous stuff from among the objects on floor and drop them into the case. SOME ONE as TRAVEL AGENT happily receives it all as payment and closes the case.)

SOME ONE as TRAVEL AGENT
Paid in full. Thank you!
(hands map over to one of the OTHERS)
Bon voyage!
(heads off, with loot)

ANY ONE as MOTHER
Wait! Aren't you coming with us?

SOME ONE as TRAVEL AGENT
No.

ONES
WHY NOT?

SOME ONE as TRAVEL AGENT
It's your vacation, not mine.

EACH ONE as FATHER
But we don't know where we're going!

SOME ONE as TRAVEL AGENT
Neither do I!

*(SOME ONE exits scene; removes
costume pieces, leaves case and receives BOOK
from STUFF without knowing how or why.)*

OTHER ONE
Now what?

*(SOME ONE turns the pages of the book
frantically looking for what happens next.)*

SOME ONE
The pages are empty – until we fill them!

OTHER ONE

How? With what?

> *(Through the rest of the story, SOME ONE
> continues to turn pages of the book, in
> amazement, reading their adventures even as
> they live them, occasionally sharing with
> another FAMILY member the fact that what's
> happening is recording itself. But now, ONES
> gather around SOMEONE to check out BOOK
> for clues to the unwritten story.)*

M.C. (may be offstage voice)

Never fear! Where there's stuff, there's story. This family
needs a Tour Guide.

> *(STUFF grabs EVERY ONE's hands and spins
> her around; as she lets go, she continues
> twirling until she's in position in front of ONES.)*

EVERY ONE as TOUR GUIDE
> *(in a quasi-French accent.)*

Hallo, Familee. I am ze tour guide.

ANY ONE as MOTHER
> *(adding sunglasses and perhaps a costume piece
> to EVERYONE's TOUR GUIDE look)*

Thank goodness!

EVERY ONE as TOUR GUIDE

Where would ze familee like to go?

ANY ONE as MOTHER

Well, it's . . . uhhhh . . .
> *(at a loss, looks to EACH ONE and OTHER
> ONE, who stare back, stumped)*

                    EACH ONE as FATHER
It's kinda. . . ?

                    OTHER ONE as EENY
It's sorta . . . ?

                    EVERY ONE as TOUR GUIDE
Yez . . . ? Eet'z wella kinda sorta what?

                    SOME ONE as MINEY
The travel agent never actually told us.

                    EVERY ONE as TOUR GUIDE
You pay ze agent for ze tour, but you do not know where ze
tour iz going?

                    SOME ONE as MINEY
That pretty much sums it up.

                    EACH ONE as FATHER
It's supposed to be exclusive –

                    ANY ONE as MOTHER
Extremely.

                    EACH ONE as FATHER
Inclusive –

                    ANY ONE as MOTHER
Incredibly.

                    EACH ONE as FATHER
And conducive.

                    ANY ONE as MOTHER
Consistently.

EVERY ONE as TOUR GUIDE
Ah! Zat tour! Why deed you not zay zo?

ANY ONE as MOTHER
We just did . . . didn't we?

EVERY ONE as TOUR GUIDE
(dances about the stage with each change of destination)
Zat tour begeenz at ze zoo.

OTHER ONE as EENY
Yaaaaaayyy!

EVERY ONE as TOUR GUIDE
Or perhaps it begeenz at ze beach?

ANY ONE as MOTHER
Ahhhhhhh!

EVERY ONE as TOUR GUIDE
Or maybe it begeenz on ze mountain?

SOME ONE as MINEY
Yesssssss!

EVERY ONE as TOUR GUIDE
Or maybe it begeenz in ze city.

SOME ONE as MINEY
(stops EVERY ONE as TOUR GUIDE in mid-flit)
Wait! You don't know where the tour begins?

EVERY ONE as TOUR GUIDE
How could I know zuch a teeng?

EACH ONE as FATHER
You've never taken the tour.

EVERY ONE as TOUR GUIDE
Of course I have not. Zis tour haz nevair been taken.

ANY ONE as MOTHER
Because it's . . . exclusive.

EACH ONE as FATHER
Extremely.

SOMEONE as MINEY
Which means . . .
          (indicating FAMILY)
. . . it's ours alone.

EVERY ONE as TOUR GUIDE
Zat ees correct.

ANY ONE as MOTHER
But you are a tour guide?

EVERY ONE as TOUR GUIDE
Wizout ze zlightest doubt.

SOME ONE as MINEY
          (handing EVERY ONE as TOUR GUIDE the
          steering wheel)
Then I say: Start guiding!

          (ANY ONE picks up the license plate and hands
          it to OTHER ONE in exchange for the two
          dolls. FAMILY lines up behind EVERY ONE as
          TOUR GUIDE, steering as if in a tour bus.
          EACH ONE plays the horn or bell, ANY ONE
          carries the dolls, SOME ONE still clutches the

book, and OTHER ONE brings up the rear,
traveling backward and displaying the license
plate.)

EVERY ONE as TOUR GUIDE
Right zis way.

ANY ONE as MOTHER
Our vacation has begun!

EACH ONE as FATHER
At last!

ALL
(including dolls)
Yaaaayyyyy!

(Dancing with the steering wheel to the rhythms
generated by EACH ONE, EVERY ONE
as TOUR GUIDE leads FAMILY around the
stage in one large sweep and then ever smaller
circles. STUFF enjoys the rhythm and dance,
too, while observing and dodging out of the
way. FAMILY starts out in high spirits, but, in
spite of EVERY ONE as TOUR GUIDE's
unwavering enthusiasm, become increasingly
puzzled, concerned, annoyed, and tired as the
road trip continues – and shrinks in scope.
About halfway to the center of the spiraling
circles, ANY ONE stops short, causing a pile-
up.)

ANY ONE as MOTHER
STOP!

(SOUNDS stop. EVERY ONE as TOUR
GUIDE and ONES stop.)

EVERY ONE as TOUR GUIDE
Iz zair ze problem?

ANY ONE as MOTHER
We're going around in circles!

EVERY ONE as TOUR GUIDE
Yayz.

ANY ONE as MOTHER
Smaller and smaller circles.

EVERY ONE as TOUR GUIDE
Yayz. We are traveling in ze very best of circlez.

ANY ONE as MOTHER
Oh. Well, I suppose that's all right, then.

EVERY ONE as TOUR GUIDE
Yayz.

EACH ONE as FATHER
(to EVERY ONE as TOUR GUIDE)
But are you sure you know which way we're headed?

EVERY ONE as TOUR GUIDE
Wizout ze zlightest doubt.

*(During the following exchange of dialogue,
EACH ONE punctuates every "zis way" with a
PING and "zat way" with a CLUNK or similar
alternating SOUNDS, using available stuff.
EVERY ONE as TOUR GUIDE sweeps an arm
to the left)*

We are headed *zis* way.

ANY ONE as MOTHER
*(repeating EVERY ONE as TOUR
GUIDE'S sweeping gesture)*
But why are we headed *zis* way?

EVERY ONE as TOUR GUIDE
(gesturing in the opposite direction)
Becauze we are not headed *zat* way.

ANY ONE as MOTHER
(mimicking second gesture)
But why aren't we headed *zat* way?

EVERY ONE as TOUR GUIDE
*(demonstrating the difference between the
gestures)*
Becauze if we are headed ZIS way . . . we cannot go ZAT
way.

ANY ONE as MOTHER
But why not?

EVERY ONE as TOUR GUIDE
*(getting concerned, but patiently repeating
gestures)*
Because zis way . . . is zis way . . . and zat way . . . is zat
way.

ANY ONE as MOTHER
I know. But if we --
(looking right --)
why are we --
(looking left --)
why can't we . . . ?
(beat)
I don't understand.

EVERY ONE as TOUR GUIDE
I do not underztand what you do not underztand.

OTHER ONE as EENY
COULD WE PLEASE JUST GO ON?

EVERY ONE as TOUR GUIDE
But of courze.

ALL
*(less enthusiastically, as ANY ONE
bounces dolls, also less enthusiastically)*
Yaaaayyy!

*(EACH ONE resumes SOUNDS of travel, as
before. EVERY ONE as TOUR GUIDE and
FAMILY continue in smaller circles
with steering wheel, dolls, and license plate,
until they're shuffling as fast as they can in a
tight spin at center.)*

OTHER ONE as EENY
Are we there yet?

EVERY ONE as TOUR GUIDE
Not yet.
*(They continue shuffling furiously for another
revolution or two or three.)*

OTHER ONE as EENY
ARE WE THERE YET?

EVERY ONE as TOUR GUIDE
NOT YET.
*(They continue shuffling furiously for another
revolution or two or three.)*

> OTHER ONE as EENY
ARE WE THERE YET?

> EVERY ONE as TOUR GUIDE
NOT YET.

> > *(They continue shuffling furiously for a few more
> > revolutions. Then OTHER ONE notices sign
> > and tries a new tactic.)*

> OTHER ONE as EENY
STOP!

> > *(EVERY ONE as TOUR GUIDE and
> > FAMILY stop. SOUNDS stop. OTHER ONE
> > indicates sign —)*

If we're not *there yet*, are we *here . . . now*?

> EVERY ONE as TOUR GUIDE
> > *(mimes rolling down a window and looking
> > around; sees sign)*
Yayz! I would zay zo!

> EVERY ONE as TOUR GUIDE and FAMILY
> > *(leaping out of "car" formation)*
YAAAYYYYY!

> > *(STUFF slips BOOK out of SOME ONE's hand
> > and opens it. Out comes the SOUND of a lion's
> > roar.)*

> EACH ONE as FATHER
What was that?

OTHER ONE as EENY
(excited at the prospect)
It sounded like a lion!
(EACH ONE gleefully takes on LION's role.)

EACH ONE as LION
RRRRROOOOAAAAARRRRRR!

*(EVERY ONE as TOUR GUIDE and SOME
ONE shriek and crouch down in a tight huddle,
yanking OTHER ONE down with them and
hiding their eyes while trembling in fright.
STUFF may join them, though they don't know
it. ANY ONE quickly tosses a costume piece or
two onto EACH ONE as LION before joining the
huddle.)*

EVERY ONE as MEENY
(from deep in the huddle)
Somebody do something!

OTHER ONE as EENY
I will!

*(cautiously crosses to stand in front of SOME
ONE as LION, offering the back of a hand to
sniff, as if to a strange dog.)*

Nice Mr. Lion . . . good Mr. Lion . . . I won't hurt you, Mr.
Lion . . .

EACH ONE as LION
*(sniffs hand, then, less aggressively, but still
troubled --)*
Roooooowwwwwwwwrrrrrrrrrrrrr!

45

(EVERY ONE as TOUR GUIDE, SOME ONE,
ANY ONE, and STUFF look on in amazement;
ALL except STUFF emit a tiny, cringing,
muted, group scream --)

EVERY ONE, SOME ONE, ANY ONE
Ahhhhhhhhh!

OTHER ONE as EENY
(scratching EACH ONE as LION under the
chin)
There, there, Mr. Lion. There, there . . .

EACH ONE as LION
(A beat, then with a sorrowful gaze into OTHER
ONE'S eyes and a pitiful tone)
Meeeeoooooowwwwwwrrrrrrrrrr!

EVERY ONE, SOME ONE, ANY ONE
(melting)
Awwwwwww . . .

OTHER ONE as EENY
(kneeling and putting an arm around EACH
ONE as LION)
Poor Mr. Lion! What's wrong?

EACH ONE as LION
Meeeeoooooowwwwwwrrrrrrrrrr!

OTHER ONE as EENY
Do you have a thorn in your paw?

EACH ONE as LION
(shaking his/her head "no")
Meeeeoooooowwwwwwrrrrrrrrrrr!

OTHER ONE as EENY
Have you been frightened by a mouse?

EACH ONE as LION
(a bit offended)
Meeeeeooooowwwwwwwrrrrrrrrr!

OTHER ONE as EENY
Then why are you so unhappy, Mr. Lion?

EACH ONE as LION
Meeeeooooowwwwwwrrrrrrr!

EVERY ONE as MEENY
Has somebody stolen his cornbread?

EACH ONE as LION
(vigorously nodding "yes")
MEEEEOOOOOWWWWW!

ANY ONE as MOTHER
(to EVERY ONE)
How on earth did you guess that?

EVERY ONE as MEENY
No one wants their cornbread stolen.

EACH ONE as LION
(shaking head in agreement)
Meeeeoooooowwwwwwwww!

OTHER ONE as EENY
Well, don't you worry, Mr. Lion. We'll find your cornbread.

SOME ONE as MINEY
Hold on! Let's not make hasty promises here!

OTHER ONE as EENY

Why not?

ANY ONE as MOTHER
*(approaching with dolls, who also befriend
EACH ONE as LION)*

Poor Mr. Lion. We will find your cornbread. We will!

SOME ONE as MINEY

How can we possibly find stolen cornbread?

OTHER ONE as EENY

We can try, can't we?

SOME ONE as MINEY

But it's probably been eaten!

OTHER ONE as EENY

Mr. Lion, have you by any chance already eaten your cornbread?

EACH ONE as LION

Meeee-yyyyyowwww?

SOME ONE as MINEY

He doesn't seem entirely sure.

ANY ONE as MOTHER

No problem.

*(ANY ONE hands dolls to OTHER ONE, picks
up stethoscope, puts it in his/her ears and holds
the receiving end toward EACH ONE as LION'S
mouth, then listens intently.)*

Open wide and say "Ahhhh!"

EACH ONE as LION
AAAAAAAAHHHHHHHHH!

ANY ONE as MOTHER
*(removes stethoscope from ears and hangs it
around his/her neck)*
No indication of cornbread.
(beat)
Tour Guide, can you guide us?

EVERY ONE as TOUR GUIDE
Along ze trail of cornbread crumbz?

ANY ONE as MOTHER
That'd work!

EVERY ONE as TOUR GUIDE
Not in ze job dezcription. Zorry.

SOME ONE as MINEY
Are you sure you're a tour guide?

EVERY ONE as TOUR GUIDE
I am ze tour guide now.

SOME ONE as MINEY
What were you before?

EVERY ONE as TOUR GUIDE
Before what?

SOME ONE as MINEY
Before NOW!

EVERY ONE as TOUR GUIDE
Ah. I was ze lawyer.

ANY ONE as MOTHER
A lawyer!

EVERY ONE as TOUR GUIDE
Zat was ze case.

ANY ONE as MOTHER
And before that?

EVERY ONE as TOUR GUIDE
Zat what?

ANY ONE as MOTHER
Zat JOB! I mean, *THAT job*!

EVERY ONE as TOUR GUIDE
Ah. I was ze taxi driver.

SOME ONE as MINEY
A taxi driver, a lawyer, and a tour guide? Really?

EVERY ONE as TOUR GUIDE
People can change.

SOME ONE as MINEY
Especially you!

EVERY ONE as TOUR GUIDE
(taking this as a compliment)
Zank you.

ANY ONE as MOTHER
*(pulling SOME ONE off to the side and speaking
confidentially)*
Are you thinking what I'm thinking?

SOME ONE as MINEY
I don't know. What are you thinking?

ANY ONE as MOTHER
I'm thinking we'd be better off going it alone.

SOME ONE as MINEY
Oh. I was thinking I'd really like a piece of cornbread.

ANY ONE as MOTHER
How about we go it alone now, with cornbread to follow?

SOME ONE as MINEY
Deal!
> *(to EVERY ONE as TOUR GUIDE, while taking*
> *back steering wheel)*
Ahem. We are very sorry to inform you that we no longer
require your services.

EVERY ONE as TOUR GUIDE
You do not need ze tour guide?

SOME ONE
That is correct. I'm very sorry, but --

EVERY ONE as TOUR GUIDE
Do not be zorry! I am glad to hear zees newz! I am off to
ze new career . . . in ze ballet!
> *(exits scene, dancing)*
Ta-ta!

SOME ONE, ANY ONE, OTHER ONE (and dolls)
Ta-ta!

OTHER ONE as EENY
(to EACH ONE as LION)
You wait here, Mr. Lion. If your cornbread can be found, we
will find it!

EACH ONE as LION
(giving them a big send-off)
RRRRRRROOAAAAWWWWWRRRRR!

ANY ONE as MOTHER
Good-bye for now.

EVERY ONE as MEENY
Let's go!

> *(As SOME ONE, ANY ONE, and OTHER ONE*
> *wave goodbye and reassemble at center*
> *with BOOK, steering wheel, dolls, and license*
> *plate, EVERY ONE and EACH ONE put*
> *aside TOUR GUIDE and LION gear and rejoin*
> *them. EACH ONE creates car and bell or*
> *horn SOUNDS and EVERY ONE leads the*
> *dance as FAMILY resumes car formation and*
> *retrace their route quickly in a reverse spiral*
> *from tiny circle to broad sweep of the stage.*
> *Meanwhile, STUFF hauls a tree stump out of the*
> *dumpster and places it directly in their route,*
> *then steps back, eager to see what happens*
> *next.)*

ANY ONE as MOTHER
STOP!

> *(FAMILY squeals to a stop in front of stump.*
> *SOME ONE dives behind stump and comes up*
> *holding PUPPET CURLY and PUPPET MOE,*
> *who both wear fright wigs. ANY ONE quickly*

52

puts a fright wig on SOME ONE, who becomes
LARRY while also operating and voicing
PUPPET CURLY and PUPPET MOE.)

SOME ONE as LARRY
(greeting FAMILY)
Hey, there!

SOME ONE as CURLY
Hi, there!

SOME ONE as PUPPET MOE
Woof-woof!

ONES
Hey!

EACH ONE as FATHER
Who – or what – are you?

SOME ONE as LARRY
Name's Larry.
(indicating PUPPET CURLY)
This here's my brother, Curly.

SOME ONE as PUPPET CURLY
Yo!

SOME ONE as LARRY
(indicating PUPPET MOE)
This here's my dog, Moe.

SOME ONE as PUPPET MOE
Woof!

OTHER ONE as EENY
Your dog!

>*(hands license plate to EVERY ONE and reaches out for PUPPET MOE.)*

Moe!

SOME ONE as PUPPET MOE
Woof! Woof!
>*(SOME ONE gives PUPPET MOE to OTHER ONE, who is entranced.)*

OTHER ONE as EENY
Oh, Moe!

SOME ONE as LARRY
Live in a tree stump.

SOME ONE as CURLY
Don't get out much.

ANY ONE as MOTHER
Pleased to meet you.

SOME ONE as LARRY
Likewise.

ANY ONE as MOTHER
Have you come across any cornbread lately?

SOME ONE as LARRY
Are you offering?

ANY ONE as MOTHER
No, we're searching!
>*(puts stethoscope in ears, holds receiving end up to SOME ONE as LARRY'S mouth)*

Open wide and say AHHHHH!

SOME ONE as LARRY
(as ANY ONE "examines" as before)
AHHHHHHH!

ANY ONE as MOTHER
(to PUPPET CURLY)
You, too.

SOME ONE as PUPPET CURLY
(same business)
AHHHHHHH!

ANY ONE as MOTHER
(to PUPPET MOE)
And you.

OTHER ONE as PUPPET MOE
(same business)
AHHHHHHH!

ANY ONE as MOTHER
Hmm. All clean.
(hangs stethoscope around neck again)

SOME ONE as LARRY
Mighty clean. Swim in a lake.

EVERY ONE as MEENY
A lake? Where?

SOME ONE as LARRY
Right here.

EVERY ONE as MEENY
I don't see a lake.

                    SOME ONE as PUPPET CURLY
Comes and goes.

                    EACH ONE as FATHER
How can a lake come and go?

                    SOME ONE as LARRY
Magic.

                    OTHER ONE as EENY
A magical lake?

                    SOME ONE as PUPPET CURLY
Black.

                    ANY ONE as MOTHER
Black magic?

                    SOME ONE as LARRY
Black coffee.

                    EACH ONE as FATHER
A black coffee lake?   Are you sure it isn't just a big mud
puddle? A puddle that comes and goes with the rain?

                    SOME ONE as LARRY
No. It's coffee.

                    SOME ONE as PUPPET CURLY
And it changes us.

                    EACH ONE as FATHER
Changes you how?

                    SOME ONE as LARRY
Don't know how.

EACH ONE as FATHER
I mean, changes you into what?

SOME ONE as PUPPET CURLY
Don't know what.

SOME ONE as LARRY
Always different.

SOME ONE as PUPPET CURLY
A monkey once.

SOME ONE as LARRY
A slug once.

SOME ONE as PUPPET CURLY
Whatever.

SOME ONE as LARRY
Whenever.

SOME ONE as PUPPET CURLY
However.

SOME ONE as LARRY
Whyever.

SOME ONE as PUPPET CURLY
Whoever.

SOME ONE as LARRY
And sometimes back.

SOME ONE as PUPPET CURLY
And sometimes forth.

                    SOME ONE as LARRY
And back.

                    SOME ONE as PUPPET CURLY
And forth.

                    SOME ONE as LARRY
And back.

                    SOME ONE as PUPPET CURLY
And forth --

                    EACH ONE as FATHER
                    (interrupting)
Can we see this magical lake?

                    SOME ONE as LARRY
Sure.

                    SOME ONE as PUPPET CURLY
Why not?

        EACH ONE, OTHER ONE, ANY ONE, EVERY ONE
                    (accompanied in cheer by dolls and PUPPET
                    MOE)
Yaaaayy --

                    SOME ONE as LARRY
                    (gently but firmly)
Must take Moe now.

                    OTHER ONE as EENY
Oh, no!
                    (reluctantly hands over PUPPET MOE, then
                    turns away to be comforted by ANY ONE.)

58

SOME ONE as LARRY

Sorry!

OTHER ONE as EENY

No Moe!

ANY ONE as MOTHER

No Moe.
(to distract and encourage OTHER ONE)
Come on, let's check out this black coffee lake!

*(As SOME ONE as LARRY, with PUPPET
CURLY and PUPPET MOE, climbs onto the tree
stump, STUFF hauls a long, dark strip of cloth
out of dumpster to create the waves of the lake.
EVERY ONE takes one end of the strip to make
waves. EACH ONE finds stuff to make water
SOUNDS. ANY ONE gives OTHER ONE the
dolls as comfort. SOME ONE as LARRY, with
PUPPET CURLY and PUPPET MOE jumps into
the lake.)*

SOMEONE as LARRY

Here we goooooooo!

*(SOMEONE as LARRY bobs for a bit, with ad
libbed shouts, barks, and splashes, then
disappears beneath the waves. EVERY ONE
continues making waves. STUFF and/or M.C.
may help make waves.)*

ANY ONE as MOTHER

Oh, my goodness! Larry jumped into the lake!

OTHER ONE as EENY

With Curly and Moe!

ANY ONE as MOTHER

They're gone!

> *(SOME ONE retrieves BOOK, opens it, and the
> Whale SOUND emerges. EACH ONE dives into
> the lake with a shout and raises PUPPET
> WHALE to the surface of the waves.)*

OTHER ONE as EENY
(brightening)

Look! A whale!

ANY ONE as MOTHER

Did the lake turn Larry, Curly, and Moe into a whale?

SOME ONE
*(flips through BOOK, but it doesn't have the
answer)*

There's no way of knowing.

OTHER ONE as EENY

Wow! It *is* magical!
> *(EACH ONE as PUPPET WHALE moans
> loudly.)*

ANY ONE as MOTHER
*(with stethoscope in ears and other end extended
toward PUPPET WHALE as it circles)*

Hush! I think I'm picking up a trace . . .

EVERY ONE as MEENY

Of cornbread?

ANY ONE as MOTHER
(nodding, but still "listening")

Could very well be.

OTHER ONE as EENY
What would a whale want with cornbread?
>   *(EACH ONE as WHALE moans and backs away,*
>   *obviously guilty.)*

ANY ONE as MOTHER
That whale looks guilty.
>   *(beat)*
I'm going in!

OTHER ONE as EENY
>   *(handing off dolls)*
Me, too!

>   *(ANY ONE, with stethoscope, and OTHER*
>   *ONE, make a run for the tree stump and jump*
>   *into the lake with much whooping and flailing.*
>   *PUPPET WHALE swims away, moaning*
>   *frantically and guiltily – with ANY ONE and*
>   *OTHER ONE, and in pursuit in a wild water*
>   *ballet. At last, ANY ONE catches up to and*
>   *grabs WHALE'S head, perhaps by the lip.*
>   *OTHER ONE catches hold at the tail end and*
>   *bobs along.)*

ANY ONE as MOTHER
I've got its head!

OTHER ONE as EENY
I've got its tail!

ANY ONE as MOTHER
>   *(wielding stethoscope)*
Open wide, whale! Say "AHHHHHHH!"

EACH ONE as PUPPET WHALE
(opening wide)
AHHHHHHHHHHHHHHH!

ANY ONE as MOTHER
(attempts to "listen" with stethoscope, but is instead sucked into PUPPET WHALE's mouth)
AHHHHHHHHHHHHHHHGGGGGGGHHHHHHHH!
(Moaning SOUND abruptly ends in a loud gulp. ANY ONE is hidden beneath the waves.)

OTHER ONE as EENY
Oh, no! She's in the belly of the whale!

EVERY ONE as MEENY
With the cornbread!
(OTHER ONE hangs on to PUPPET WHALE for dear life, bobbing in the waves.)

SOME ONE as MINEY
(from shore)
Can you hear us in there?

ANY ONE as MOTHER (unseen)
Yes!

EACH ONE as PUPPET WHALE
(burping loudly, with embarrassment)
BRRRRRRUUUUPPPPPPPP!

EVERY ONE as MEENY
Ewwwww! Whale burp!

OTHER ONE as EENY
Other than that, it seems to be a very nice whale.

                    SOME ONE as MINEY
That burping whale ate our mother!

                    OTHER ONE as EENY
Well, other than that, too.

                    SOME ONE as MINEY
                    (from shore)
What's it like in there?

                    ANY ONE as MOTHER(unseen)
Come see for yourself.

                    SOME ONE as MINEY
No, thank you. Just wondering.

                    EACH ONE as PUPPET WHALE
                    (same business)
BRRRRRRUUUPPPPPPPPP!

                    EVERY ONE as MEENY
EWWWWWWW! Another whale burp!

                    OTHER ONE as EENY
Nice whale. Easy, whale.

                    ANY ONE as MOTHER (unseen)
So . . . here's the good news –

                    SOME ONE as MINEY
There's good news?

                    ANY ONE as MOTHER (unseen)
Yes. There's cornbread in here!

    EVERY ONE as MEENY and OTHER ONE as EENY
Yaaayyyy!

SOME ONE as MINEY
Never mind the cornbread! There's YOU in there!

ANY ONE as MOTHER (unseen)
Well, that's the bad news.

EVERY ONE as MEENY
And the cornbread's already been digested, hasn't it?

ANY ONE as MOTHER (unseen)
Um . . . yesssss . . . pretty much.

SOME ONE as MINEY
Enough with the cornbread! We're going to get you out!

ANY ONE (offstage voice)
I'd appreciate that.

SOME ONE as MINEY
LET HER OUT, WHALE!

EACH ONE as PUPPET WHALE
(wants to help, but responds with burping
SOUND)
BRRRRRUUUUUUUPPPPPPPPP!

EVERY ONE as MEENY
EEEEEWWWWWW! More whale burp!

OTHER ONE as EENY
Good whale! Good try!

EVERY ONE as MEENY
Not good enough.

SOME ONE as MINEY
COUGH, WHALE!

EACH ONE as PUPPET WHALE
BRRRRECCCCH! BRRRRRECCCCCCH! BRECK-
BRECK-BRECK!

EVERY ONE as MEENY
EWWWWWWW-- ! Whale cough!

OTHER ONE as EENY
Stop that! The whale is trying to help!

EVERY ONE as MEENY
But it's not doing any good --

SOME ONE as MINEY
(growing more frantic --)
SNEEZE, WHALE!

EACH ONE as WHALE
AAAAAAAAHHHHHHHHH-
BRRRRRUUUUCCCCHHHHHHHHHOOOOOOOOO!

EVERY ONE as MEENY
EWWWWWWW--! Whale sneeze!

OTHER ONE as EENY
(to EVERY ONE)
SHUSH!
(to WHALE)
Way to go, Whale!

EVERY ONE as MEENY
Way to go where? Nothing's happening!

SOME ONE as MINEY
(almost at wit's end --)
THROW UP, WHALE!

EACH ONE as PUPPET WHALE
BBBBBRRUUUUUUUUKKKKKKK!
BBBBRRRRRUUUUUKKKKKKK!
BBBBRRRRUUUUCKKKKKKK!

EVERY ONE as MEENY
EWWWWWWWWWWWWWWWWWWWW -- whale
vomit!

OTHER ONE as EENY
Wait, wait, wait! Maybe that did it . . . ?
(a beat, but hope quickly turns to despair)

EVERY ONE as MEENY
Nothing. Not even cornbread.

OTHER ONE as EENY
Poor whale.

ANY ONE as MOTHER (unseen)
Poor me!

EVERY ONE as MEENY
Poor everybody!

SOME ONE as MINEY
You know what? If this weren't so tragic, it'd be kinda
funny.

*(SOME ONE, OTHER ONE, and EVERY
ONE look at one another. A beat, then smiles
dawn, and nods grow more vigorous as a
solution strikes them all simultaneously.)*

                    EVERY ONE and OTHER ONE
Whoa!

                    SOMEONE as MINEY
One . . . two . . . three . . .

          SOMEONE, OTHER ONE, and EVERY ONE
LAUGH, WHALE!

                    (SOME ONE, EVERY ONE and OTHER
                    ONE, with dolls, lean in on PUPPET WHALE
                    and tickle it.)

TICKLE! TICKLE! TICKLE! TICKLE!

                    EACH ONE as WHALE
BRAAAHHH-HAAAHHH-HAAAAHHH-HAAAAHHH-
HAAAAHHHH-HAAAAAHHH!   HAAAAAHHHH-
HAAAAAHHHH-HAAAAAAAHHH!

                    ANY ONE as MOTHER
                    (emerging)
I'm out!

                    EACH ONE as WHALE
                    (a sigh of relief)
WHOOOOOOooooooooo . . .

          SOME ONE, EVERY ONE, OTHER ONE
YAAAAYYYY!

                    (WHALE disappears into waves; ONES
                    gather in a group hug. STUFF gathers wave
                    material and returns it to container.)

M.C. (may be offstage voice)
Well, well, well. All the stuff of a happy ending . . . almost.

OTHER ONE
Goodbye, Whale!

EVERY ONE
And cornbread!

ANY ONE
And Lion.

EACH ONE
And Larry and Curley . . .

OTHER ONE
(wistfully)
Goodbye . . . Moe.

SOME ONE
Wait! There needs to be a little more . . .

(pretends to read from BOOK, as ONES gather round, and STUFF, smiling, tiptoes away and disappears into the dumpster)

And so, the friendly Whale apologized for eating the Lion's cornbread and explained that it had actually been fed to him by a mischievous monkey who had since been turned into a slug by the magical lake.

EVERY ONE
(peering into book)
Is that what it says?

SOME ONE
I just made it up. But that's what it says *now.* Look . . .

*(ONES examine book. Sure enough, the story is
still appearing as it's created.
As EACH ONE, EVERY ONE, ANY ONE and
SOME ONE continue with this, OTHER ONE
slips away without their noticing to stare up
longingly at the dumpster.)*

EVERY ONE

Wow! Okay . . . well . . . add this --
(as if dictating to the book)
The family all pitched in to bake a new batch of cornbread
for the Lion . . .

ANY ONE
(dictating)
. . . who was as touched and grateful as he was hungry.

EVERY ONE
(dictating)
Then they baked more cornbread and shared it all around.

EACH ONE

Really?

EVERY ONE
(Indicating BOOK)
Check it out.

EACH ONE
(checks BOOK; it's there)
Nice!

EVERY ONE
(dictating)
You can never have too much cornbread.

SOME ONE
(pretending to read)
And after a fond farewell, the family found their way home,
convinced that this vacation tour had been everything it was
promised to be – extremely exclusive, incredibly inclusive,
and consistently conducive --

ANY ONE
. . . to fun . . .

EACH ONE
. . . and friendship . . .

EVERY ONE
. . . and cornbread.

SOME ONE
(closes BOOK, laughing)
The end.

M.C. (may be offstage voice)
Also known as . . . the beginning.

EACH ONE
Best story I've ever read . . .

SOME ONE
. . . or written.

ANY ONE
It needs a title. What should we call it?

EVERY ONE
It's kind of weird. It's got all that stuff in it.

EACH ONE
Bits and pieces of all of us.

SOME ONE
"STUFF! A Curious Collection."

ANY ONE
That's it!

EACH ONE
Perfect.

ANY ONE
It'd be fun to illustrate. I'm already seeing sketches in my head.

SOME ONE
(handing BOOK to ANY ONE)
Feel free!

ANY ONE
Really?

SOME ONE
Why not?

EACH ONE
There could be music . . . "The Lion's Song". . . "The Whale's Song" . . .

EVERY ONE
We could do a musical! With singing and dancing!

ANY ONE
And costumes! And scenery!

SOME ONE
At the library! Do any of you hang out at the library?

ANY ONE

Sure.

EACH ONE

We've probably all walked right past one another.

EVERY ONE

Let's not do that anymore.

SOME ONE

Deal!

SOME ONE, EACH ONE, EVERY ONE, ANY ONE
(as all four put their hands together in the center of their circle)

Deal!

(Suddenly, they notice OTHER ONE, all alone at the dumpster, and abruptly stop in surprise, hands still joined.)

EACH ONE

Look!

ANY ONE

Shhhhhh!

SOME ONE
(whispering)

What's going on?

EVERY ONE
(whispering)

Listen!

OTHER ONE
(shyly calling up to the top of container --)

Moe?
(a beat, then a little louder)

Moe?
(a beat, then, full out --)

I miss you, Moe!
(a beat, then --)

I love you, Moe!

*(PUPPET MOE appears at the top of dumpster
OTHER ONE reaches upward, PUPPET MOE
drops into OTHER ONE'S hands. OTHER ONE
hugs PUPPET MOE, dances around joyfully to
the approval of the remaining ONES.)*

Moe-Moe-Moe! I love you. I *love* you!
(as PUPPET MOE --)

Woof-woof! Woof-woof!

SOME ONE, EVERY ONE, EACH ONE, ANY ONE
(raising joined hands to cheer)

Yaaaayyyy!
(STUFF and M.C. peer out to watch.)

OTHER ONE
(to ONES -- and to PUPPET MOE)

I think . . . I'm ready . . . I think . . . maybe . . . I think maybe
I'm ready to think about . . . maybe . . . I think I'm ready to
think about getting a new dog.

ANY ONE

Yes! Think about it!
*(ALL nod in agreement. ANY ONE and OTHER
ONE hug.)*

SOME ONE
Well. We should probably be getting home.

ANY ONE
I'll walk with you.

EACH ONE
Me, too.

EVERY ONE
Me, three.

OTHER ONE
Me, four.
                    (as PUPPET MOE)
Woof! Woof!

ANY ONE
                    (indicating BOOK)
Are we taking this with us?

SOME ONE
Of course. It's our story.

                    *(ANY ONE opens BOOK. MELODY plays.
                    ONES exit together as friends. MELODY fades.
                    STUFF watches them go, fondly, then, with a
                    last wave toward audience, disappears into
                    dumpster.)*

M.C.
                    (re-entering, if previously offstage --)
And so it is that we reconnect . . . and rejoice.
                    *(turning the sign back to ANY PLACE. ANY
                    TIME.)*
Time to go. Thank you for joining us.
                    (beat)

M.C. (CONT)
Don't forget your stuff.

*(MELODY plays. M.C. bows and exits.
MELODY fades. End of play.)*

www.ingramcontent.com/pod-product-compliance
Lightning Source LLC
Chambersburg PA
CBHW031229120626
46545CB00003B/1053